Advent 2024

DAILY REFLECTIONS, PRACTICES & PRAYERS

Becoming Pilgrims of HOPE

JANET SCHAEFFLER, OP

23rd TWENTY-THIRD PUBLICATIONS
twentythirdpublications.com

Twenty-Third Publications
977 Hartford Turnpike, Unit A
Waterford, CT 06385
(860) 437-3012 or (800) 321-0411
twentythirdpublications.com

ISBN: 978-1-62785-816-8

Image credits: front cover, shutterstock.com/Bobby Stevens Photo; back cover, stock.adobe.com/Adam Ján Figel'

Printed in the U.S.A.

bayard A division of Bayard, Inc.

Pilgrims of Hope

This year, when we conclude Advent, the universal Church will begin the 2025 Holy Year. A Jubilee or Holy Year is a time of prayer, pilgrimage, and acts of mercy, built on the Old Testament tradition of a jubilee year of rest, forgiveness, and renewal.

Holy Years first began in 1300; since 1490, they have been celebrated every twenty-five years. The last ordinary jubilee was the Great Jubilee of 2000.

Special anniversaries have called for extraordinary holy years: 1933 to mark the 1900th anniversary of Jesus' death and resurrection, and 1983 for the 1950th anniversary. In 2015-2016, we saw an extraordinary Year of Mercy, emphasizing mercy and the need for the Church to keep alive the spirit of the Second Vatican Council.

The motto given to this Holy Year 2025 by Pope Francis is "Pilgrims of Hope," in the belief that the year "can contribute greatly to restoring a climate of hope and trust as a prelude to the renewal and rebirth that we so urgently desire" after years of pandemic and suffering.

This sacred Advent season—preparing us, once again, for the celebration of Jesus coming into our world—is also a unique time: preparing us to reflect on and live in hope. We can be hopeful people because Jesus modeled it for us. In this time and place, we are now called to deepen hope, to be people of trust, to be pilgrims and messengers of hope in all the circumstances of our lives.

Janet Schaeffler, OP

Jeremiah 33:14–16; 1 Thessalonians 3:12—4:2; Luke 21:25–28, 34–36

Hope-Filled Promises

I will fulfill the promise I made.

JEREMIAH 33:14

One stormy night when an elderly couple asked for a room, the clerk said the hotel was full. He insisted that the couple take his room. While checking out, the elderly man said, "You're the kind of man who should be managing the country's best hotel. Someday I'll build you one." A few years later, the clerk received a letter and an airline ticket to New York. Upon his arrival, his host took him to a magnificent building at 5th Avenue and 34th Street, saying, "This is the hotel I built for you to manage." The man was William Waldorf Astor; the hotel was the Waldorf Astoria.

The riches that come from promises kept! Jeremiah ushers us into Advent with hope and assurance. God promises the people of Jeremiah's time that new life will come, that there will be safety and justice after suffering years of danger and discrimination.

What promises does God makes to us today? According to Jeremiah, God will bring new life out of the places we think are hopeless.

DAILY PRACTICE: Even though, at times, it might seem that God's promises take a long time to come, begin this Advent with hope. Find one sign of hope each day of Advent.

ADVENT PRAYER: *Because of your compassionate promises, Generous God, I begin my Advent journey with hope. Help me to remember who you are: always trustworthy, ever present.*

Isaiah 2:1–5; Matthew 8:5–11

Rooted in God's Vision

"Let us go up to the LORD's mountain...that he may instruct us in his ways, and we may walk in his paths."

ISAIAH 2:3

During the Vietnam War, there was a man who stood in front of the White House every night with a candle. One evening, a reporter asked: "Do you think you're going to change the policies of this country by standing out here alone with a candle?" The man answered, "I don't stand here to change the country's policies. I stand here so the policies don't change me."

During our Advent days, as we remember the story of 2,000 years ago, we recall that Jesus came into a world immersed in attitudes and practices that needed to be challenged. At times, we may find ourselves in a culture that espouses beliefs contrary to God's ways. How do we avoid getting swept up in attitudes and actions that are in conflict with God's vision? The invitation from Isaiah today and the practice of the man with the candle in Washington, DC, are a reminder to us to intentionally anchor ourselves in God's ways.

DAILY PRACTICE: What practice helps you to deepen hope, strengthening yourself in the gospel way of seeing? Is there a new practice or attitude you could begin during this Advent?

ADVENT PRAYER: *God of Truth, lead me to search for your vision; empower me to hold on to the ways you have taught me.*

Isaiah 11:1–10; Luke 10:21–24

Seeing a Friend

Then the wolf shall be a guest of the lamb,
and the leopard shall lie down with the young goat.

ISAIAH 11:6

Richard W. Chilson, in his book *Yeshua of Nazareth*, tells of a time he was driving home on the freeway and found himself behind a slow-moving car. As he neared his exit, it was too late to pass the car. Because he was in his usual hurry, his frustration grew. Thinking all kinds of condemnations, he pulled alongside the car at the stoplight by the exit. As he glanced over, he saw a dear friend. He wrote, "Instantly the situation changed."

Today's Isaiah reading describes the peaceable kingdom, a world that only happens when we see all others as dear friends. Have there been times in your life when someone you've presumed to be your "enemy" turned out to be a dear friend? As the lion and the lamb, the leopard and the young goat experienced their similarities rather than their differences, do we realize that all of us have the same hopes, concerns, fears, and dreams—that we are one?

DAILY PRACTICE: As you see and hear about people today (especially in news stories), imagine them as your dear friend.

ADVENT PRAYER: *God who has made us one people, give me eyes to see and a heart to respond to each person (and various groups of people) as my cherished friend.*

Isaiah 25:6–10a; Matthew 15:29–37

Nourishing God

Then he took the seven loaves and the fish,
gave thanks, broke the loaves, and gave them to the disciples,
who in turn gave them to the crowds.

MATTHEW 15:36

Jesus ended each phase of his ministry with feeding people. His ministry in Galilee ended with the feeding of the 5,000. His ministry in the Gentile area ended with the feeding of the 4,000; his Judean ministry ended with the feeding of the disciples in the upper room. Jesus always fed people. As we recall all of Jesus' life, he also "fed" people in various ways (not just with food)—always nurturing who they were, always reaching out in nourishment with what they needed.

The Incarnation—God becoming one of us—happened so that God could teach us how to live as humans. Today's gospel story (along with many others) of feeding and nourishing speaks of one of the most crucial attributes of God: compassion. God suffers with us and feels our pain; God never leaves but comforts and strengthens us.

DAILY PRACTICE: As you reflect upon yesterday, last week, or last month, when were you in pain? When were you worried? When were you "hungry" for something? Can you recall how God fed and nourished you during those times?

ADVENT PRAYER: *Compassionate God, you continually surround me with care, generosity, and strength. In gratitude, help me to be like you—nourishing those in need, offering comfort and kindness.*

Isaiah 26:1-6; Matthew 7:21, 24-27

Abundance of Goodness

Give thanks to the LORD, for he is good.

PSALM 118:1

There's a woman in London who goes to the subway station every day and sits on the bench to listen to the recorded announcement to "Mind the gap" (the space between the train and the platform). Her husband recorded the announcement in 1950. After his death in 2003, she found this way to feel his presence. Recently, his voice was replaced by an empty electronic one. In her distress, she asked for a recording to continue listening to her husband's voice at home.

Knowing the history, the London subway transport company decided to restore the announcement at the stop near the house where the woman lives.

Today's psalm reminds us of the goodness of our God. God's goodness most dramatically (and simply) surrounds us through the people in our lives: in this story, the dedicated love of a long marriage as well as the compassionate sensitivity of the subway company.

DAILY PRACTICE: Are there instances of goodness that surround you that you sometimes don't notice or take for granted? During these Advent days, take time to notice, to be more aware. Can you also be like the subway company, showing sensitive goodness to another?

ADVENT PRAYER: *God of Goodness, your loving kindness in my life is constant. In gratitude, help me be a source of goodness in the lives of those around me.*

Isaiah 29:17–24; Matthew 9:27–31

Ecstasy of Seeing

And their eyes were opened.

MATTHEW 9:30

As a man dies, an angel begins to escort him around, taking him to places where the scenery renders him speechless. "I had no idea," the man says. He marvels at lush green valleys, rushing rivers, sunlight dancing along the landscape, an endless palette of blues in the sky and in the sea. The man tastes the invigoration of the refreshing air, drinks in majestic vistas, imposing mountain peaks, and dramatic sunsets, and fills his lungs with the earthiness of the verdant forest floors. "I am ecstatic!" he tells his host. "So, this is heaven?" "No," the angel replied, "I just wanted to make sure you had an opportunity to see all the things you missed while you lived on earth."

Many stories in Scripture, including today's, call us to attentive seeing. Do our busy, worried, preoccupied lives cause us to miss the important, the beautiful, the essentials of our gifted life and faith journey?

DAILY PRACTICE: Long before Scripture was written down, Creation spoke to us of God, revealing God's grandeur. Even if you are in the midst of cold weather, spend some time outside. What do you see that you haven't noticed before?

ADVENT PRAYER: *Wondrous God, help me to see with new eyes; remind me not to take for granted the splendor and the simplicity of all you have given us.*

Isaiah 30:19–21, 23–26; Matthew 9:35—10:1, 5a, 6–8

A Zigzag Life

His heart was moved with pity.

MATTHEW 9:36

In parts of England, you can see wavy brick walls, often called "crinkle crankle walls," the Old English version of "zigzag." Our first response is to consider them a waste of brick, yet they use fewer bricks than straight walls. Walls just one brick thick are easily toppled, so they generally have a thickness of two or more layers of bricks and are reinforced at regular intervals with vertical posts. A wavy one-brick wall can stand on its own due to the arch support provided by its shape.

These wavy walls also help fruit trees grow better. The curves create pockets that protect the trees from the wind while also trapping heat from the sun and radiating it back into the trees.

Often, we might feel that we are zigzagging when we'd rather have life be a straight, neat line. In the long run, though, will the zigzagging of life bring us fewer problems (fewer bricks) and more growth (strengthened support) as well as create pockets of protection for others?

DAILY PRACTICE: Draw a map of your life, with all its zigs and zags. Mark the times you felt God's support. Circle the times you were a pocket of protection for another.

ADVENT PRAYER: *God whose heart is always moved with compassion, my hope is in you through the zigzags of life.*

DECEMBER 8 · SECOND SUNDAY *of* **ADVENT**

Baruch 5:1–9; Philippians 1:4–6, 8–11; Luke 3:1–6

Sustaining Hope

"Every valley shall be filled...and all flesh shall see the salvation of God." LUKE 3:5–6

Fr. Pierre Teilhard de Chardin was a man of realistic hope. After a talk laying out a Scriptural vision of unity and peace for the world, he was challenged by colleagues: "That's a wonderful vision of things, but suppose we blow up the world with a nuclear bomb: what happens to your vision?" "That would set things back millions of years," de Chardin replied, "but this will still come to fruition, not because I say so or because the facts right now indicate that it will, but because God promised it and in the resurrection of Jesus has shown he delivers on his promise."

Advent calls us to hope. Yet, are there times when we doubt, mistrust, or even despair? Do we give up because we think that suffering, an injustice, an evil is so much bigger than anything we can do to turn it around? Even though we are certainly called to do our part, authentic hope lies not in us but in the steadfastness of God's promises.

DAILY PRACTICE: Choose a Scripture verse that reminds you of God's promise of hope. Whenever gloom creeps in, pray this verse, anchoring yourself in God, the source of hope.

ADVENT PRAYER: *God of Hope, even when things seem bleak, may your hope overflow in me, spilling out into the lives of those around me.*

DECEMBER 9

THE IMMACULATE CONCEPTION *of the* **BLESSED VIRGIN MARY**

Genesis 3:9–15, 20; Ephesians 1:3–6, 11–12; Luke 1:26–38

Lives Filled with Yes

"Behold, I am the handmaid of the Lord."

LUKE 1:38

A woman had a dream about her death. She held out her hands to God, proclaiming, "Look, I've done nothing wrong. My hands are clean." God replied, "Yes, but they are empty."

Mary's greatness is not really in the fact that she did no wrong but rather that she said yes to God. Mary was like us, a free human being. Mary needed to say yes and then continue living her yes during every happening of her life. It undoubtedly wasn't easy. At times, there were probably tears of hardship and questioning.

Mary's call is our call. It has been said that what we are is God's gift to us; what we become is our gift to God. Responding to God's gift to us—of our precious life, of God's promise to always be with us—what are we becoming? How often during the day do we say yes?

DAILY PRACTICE: Place a picture of open hands in a spot where you will see it often. At the end of each day, imagine: If you were to meet God in heaven today, would your hands be empty or filled with yeses to God and God's people?

ADVENT PRAYER: *God of Yes, your gifts fill me with hope. Help me respond to the daily opportunities to say yes so my hands are never empty but are filled with love.*

DECEMBER 10

TUESDAY *of the* SECOND WEEK (Our Lady of Loreto)

Isaiah 40:1–11; Matthew 18:12–14

Unwavering Unity

Sing to the Lord *a new song.*

PSALM 96:1

Today we commemorate the fifty-sixth anniversary of the death of the Trappist monk and writer Thomas Merton. He shared with us his profound experience of conversion: “In Louisville, at the corner of Fourth and Walnut, in the center of the shopping district, I was suddenly overwhelmed with the realization that I loved all these people, that they were mine and I theirs, that we could not be alien to one another even though we were total strangers.”

This reality of unity was not just a pious platitude for Merton. He wrote to his friend Dorothy Day: “I don’t feel that I can in conscience, at a time like this, go on writing just about things like meditation. I think I have to face the big issues, the life-and-death issues.”

He didn’t dismiss the importance of meditation, prayer, and liturgy, but he realized that in our lives as hope-filled disciples, those spiritual practices spill over to all we do. Does meditation compel us to realize that we are all connected and live as one family?

DAILY PRACTICE: Often, we all find ourselves at the corner of a Fourth and Walnut. How, today, will you see a stranger and view them as belonging to you?

ADVENT PRAYER: *God of Unity, help me to sing and live a new song: to see everyone—those different from me, family or friends who might be separated from me, those I encounter for only a moment—as one with me.*

DECEMBER 11

WEDNESDAY *of the* SECOND WEEK (Saint Damasus I)

Isaiah 40:25–31; Matthew 11:28–30

Message from the Routine

Do not forget all his gifts.

PSALM 103:2

A recent social media post shared, "When my daughter was visiting and passed my bedroom, she asked, 'Do you do that every day?' I replied, 'Do what?' She said, 'Make your bed and put all those pillows on.' When I answered yes, she responded, 'Why? You are the only one who sees it.' 'Oh, dear, I make my bed because it's a gift I get to open at the end of every day. A gift not everyone has. While I'm making my bed in the morning and opening it at night, I'm reminded of what a great blessing my bed is in my life. It reminds me to pray for those who do not have the gifts I have, and it challenges me to ask myself how I might share my gifts. I'm thankful for my bed.'"

Advent/Christmas, often a season of thank yous, is also a time of giving to those in need. How do we continue these practices—gratitude and giving—throughout the year?

DAILY PRACTICE: Make and unmake your bed with gratitude and an awareness of those who do not have a bed. What other habitual daily activity might remind you of your gifts and those who don't get to enjoy them?

ADVENT PRAYER: *God of all gifts, thank you—especially for things I too often take for granted. Show me new ways of sharing what I've been given.*

DECEMBER 12

THURSDAY - OUR LADY *of* GUADALUPE

Zechariah 2:14–17 or Revelation 11:19a; 12:1–6a, 10ab; Luke 1:26–38 or Luke 1:39–47

A Challenge to a New Way

"Many nations will bind themselves to the LORD on that day."

ZECHARIAH 2:15

Advent invites us to see Mary as the mother of newness because of the new life in her womb. In the beginning of the Americas, Mary would again be the mother of newness, calling these continents to build something new.

In their beginnings, the Americas—despite injustices, poverty, and wars—were unique. They welcomed people from every race, nation, and ethnicity. It is within this welcoming environment that Our Lady of Guadalupe appeared to Juan Diego in 1531. Mary challenged all peoples of this land to become a new people as reflected in her mestiza face. In her face, each would recognize elements of their own skin and ethnicity. In diversity, unity.

One of the core messages of Our Lady of Guadalupe, Patroness of the Americas, is this challenge of unity: not new territories of segregation but a newness where people of all backgrounds, colors, and ethnicities could live and work in mutual respect, peace, and harmony.

DAILY PRACTICE: Learn something new about another culture: talk with someone from another ethnic background, participate in today's services at a Hispanic parish, visit an ethnic restaurant, another church, etc.

ADVENT PRAYER: *All-embracing God, call me to newness. Help me to see each person in new ways, appreciating their uniqueness. Help me to reach out to every person in new ways, responding to their needs.*

Isaiah 48:17–19; Matthew 11:16–19

Waging Peace

If only you would attend to my commandments,
your peace would be like a river. ISAIAH 48:18

During a recent retreat, we reflected on Judyth Hill's poem "Waging Peace." The participants were invited to write their own prayers on waging peace, including a focus on the resources within them and around them, their personal tools for spreading moments of peace. Their prayers included serene patience, each new day's sunrise, unwavering persistence, fervent prayer, simple acts that change someone's day, empathetic communication, supportive community, boundless hope, radiant beauty, joyful "Good morning" text messages, attentive listening, humble apologies, respect for differences, and random acts of kindness.

Today in Isaiah, God tells us our peace will flow throughout the world when we live God's commands. What might be God's directives for you today? When you feel worried or upset, what might be God's wisdom for you? When the world around you seems chaotic or destructive, what are God's teachings and directions?

DAILY PRACTICE: Write a prayer about your commitment to wage peace. Include gratitude for and a commitment to use the helps God has placed within you and around you to bring peace.

ADVENT PRAYER: *God of Peace, when discord is within me or around me, help me to be your peace, to shine your light in the darkest corners, and to inspire others to join in your work of waging peace in a world hungry for unity, harmony, and serenity.*

Sirach 48:1-4, 9-11; Matthew 17:9a, 10-13

A New Job

Shepherd of Israel...Stir up your power, and come to save us.

PSALM 80:2-3

To help manage the season's stress, a British supermarket advertised a new job—a Christmas Light Untangler: "This new position offers you the chance to show that every little bit helps, by running the unique in-store service with a friendly approach and making a genuine difference to the little things that matter to our customers this Christmas." The first duty included "Staffing and managing the Christmas Lights Untangling stand."

There are times—not just Christmas—when we might feel that everything is jumbled, tangled, and twisted. Today's psalm reminds us that our God is our Untangler (and has had that job for eternity). Of course, God asks us to do our part: prayer, meditation, journaling, embracing change, focusing on gratitude, seeking support from others.

Perhaps one of the best ways to untangle our lives is to look around: How can we walk with others who are experiencing a life that is tangled up?

DAILY PRACTICE: On your desk or bedside table, put a sign that says "The Untangling Place" as a reminder of our provident God and your call to support others when life seems chaotic.

ADVENT PRAYER: *God our Untangler, you remind us (as in the supermarket ad) that every little bit helps. Nudge me toward the little things that will help me rely on you and support others through their hard times.*

Zephaniah 3:14–18a; Philippians 4:4–7; Luke 3:10–18

Where Is Joy?

Rejoice in the Lord always.

PHILIPPIANS 4:4

An affluent, successful man was always worried. Searching for answers, he explained his restlessness to a sage in a nearby village. The sage suggested that he return the next day, when he would tell him how to stay happy and worry-free. Approaching the hut the next day, he saw the sage looking for something outside his hermitage. When the man asked if he could help, the sage replied, "I lost my ring."

After searching for a long time with no luck, the man asked where the ring exactly fell. The sage explained, "My ring fell in the hut of the hermitage. But it is very dark there, so I am looking for the ring here outside."

The visitor expressed his astonishment and disbelief. The sage replied, "My son, this is your solution. You came with the problem that you have no shortage of anything, but you are not happy. You're looking in the wrong place."

Joy is within us. Joy is a gift from God. Whether life is going well right now or we are encountering worries and disappointments, God's presence of compassion, joy, and hope are embedded in us.

DAILY PRACTICE: End each day reflecting on the small (but never insignificant) moments of joy in your day.

ADVENT PRAYER: *God of Joy, remind me that I don't need to search for joy. Joy comes from you, from all your blessings that constantly surround me.*

Numbers 24:2–7, 15–17a; Matthew 21:23–27

Others First

He teaches the humble his way.

PSALM 25:9

Back when a sundae cost far less, a young boy asked the server its price. "Fifty cents," she replied. The boy took out a handful of change, studying his small collection of coins. "How much is a dish of plain ice cream?" he inquired. "Thirty-five cents," she said abruptly, as other customers were now waiting to be served. The boy again counted his coins, then said, "I'll have the plain ice cream, please." The server brought the ice cream and the bill and walked away. Finishing his ice cream, the boy paid the cashier and departed. When the server came back, she started wiping down the counter and then began to cry at what she saw. There, placed neatly beside the empty dish, was fifteen cents—her tip.

Today's psalm reminds us that the humble know the way of God. Humility is not putting ourselves down. Baptist pastor Rick Warren once said, "Humility is not thinking less of yourself; it is thinking of yourself less." The way of God is thinking of others first, making decisions based on what is right, what is good for the other.

DAILY PRACTICE: In these last days before Christmas, how might you respond to others' needs first: your family, the busy store clerks, people in traffic, friends who are ill, those in need?

ADVENT PRAYER: *Always-caring God, open my heart to make decisions flowing from kindness and thoughtfulness.*

Genesis 49:2, 8–10; Matthew 1:1–17

One Family

The genealogy of Jesus Christ, the son of David, the son of Abraham.

MATTHEW 1:1

For many people today, genealogy has become a serious hobby. We are curious about who we belong to.

Today we hear one of the genealogies of Jesus' family. Given those times, we would expect that Jesus' family tree would be traced through the fathers of the family. Luke's genealogy does that. Matthew, though, breaks from that pattern on four occasions (in addition to Mary) to also mention mothers (Tamar, Rahab, Ruth, and the wife of Uriah).

Because it was very rare for women to be included in a Jewish genealogy, today many speculate why Matthew did this. Perhaps one reason is that it highlights a characteristic we will see in Jesus' ministry and teachings, which continually tell us we are one family. The four women were Gentiles: Tamar and Rahab were Canaanites, Ruth was a Moabite, Bathsheba married into a Hittite household.

Even in Jesus' family tree, God incorporates the whole world, Jew and Gentile; our God is for all—every tribe and family of the earth.

DAILY PRACTICE: While celebrating with your family this season, are there others around you—perhaps different from you—that you could invite to join your family?

ADVENT PRAYER: *God of Family, God of All, I dream of the oneness that is your vision. Help me to build bridges of unity connecting me to everyone—for I belong to them.*

Jeremiah 23:5–8; Matthew 1:18–25

Dynamic Hope

I will raise up a righteous branch for David...
he shall do what is just and right. JEREMIAH 23:5

In Jeremiah, we hear God promise a new king from David's line who will rule justly. In God's vision, people are called to do something.

Saint Augustine said: "Hope has two beautiful daughters; their names are Anger and Courage. Anger at the way things are, and Courage to see that they do not remain as they are."

Hope does not let us be complacent. Even though hope is rooted in God's promises, we have a significant role. Hope is not just passive optimism; hope calls us to action and transformation.

Glenmary Fr. John Rausch (an advocate for the people of Appalachia) once said: "We in the church have got to look around rather than look up, look around to the sufferings and struggles of people and nature. When we do look up it's got to be with a plea that our hearts can be more attentive to the needs of others. God has empowered us. We can't let God take the bum rap for why things aren't done."

DAILY PRACTICE: How is your hope filled with anger and courage? What one courageous thing can you do today to bring justice and goodness?

ADVENT PRAYER: *God who empowers us, help me not only to be more attentive but to do something for the needs of others.*

Judges 13:2–7, 24–25a; Luke 1:5–25

How?

Zechariah said to the angel, "How shall I know this?"

LUKE 1:18

Why? How can this be? Are you serious? These are questions we often ask throughout life, especially in the face of surprises and challenges.

Often, we question Zechariah's faith because, on this decisive occasion, he questioned the angel. What about the rest of his life? The gospel tells us that this occurrence was preceded and followed by a life of godliness. Verse 13 also tells us that God was answering Zechariah's prayer when he promised him a son; Zechariah was a righteous and prayerful man.

We don't really know why Zechariah questioned. Maybe he was so surprised, he couldn't think straight. Perhaps—after so many years of begging for a son and receiving a "no"—he was skeptical in order to protect himself from disappointment.

Questions, wonderings, doubts, and anxieties are normal. For Zechariah, they were in the face of a wonderful surprise. Sometimes, for us, they might come because of challenges, even injustices. One of the questions this gospel poses for us is this: How do we cling to hope and the promises of God in the difficult times?

DAILY PRACTICE: Watch today for times of challenge, times of surprise. Do you question? Do your questions bring you closer to God, closer to hope-filled actions?

ADVENT PRAYER: *Answering God, thank you for listening to my questions. Help me rely on your answers; spur me toward courageous living.*

Isaiah 7:10–14; Luke 1:26–38

Look Backward

"How can this be?"

LUKE 1:34

When Mary asks, "How?" Gabriel responds oddly. After explaining that the Holy Spirit will overshadow her, he points her to the experience of her cousin. Because extended families—in those days—were very close, Mary probably already knew that Elizabeth was pregnant. The angel is not telling Mary about something that will happen but something that has already happened.

Why would Gabriel mention this if Mary already knew? For Mary, who was troubled, fearful, and perplexed, Gabriel had an important message: "Remember what God has already done." Whenever you're afraid or worried, remember all the times God has already been with you.

Often when we're immersed in doubts, anxieties, and problems, it is difficult to trust, difficult to walk through them with hope. The angel was speaking to us as well as to Mary: Look backwards. Notice all the ways, times, and places where God has been with you in the past. In those memories, be comforted in the assurance that God will never forget you in the present or future.

DAILY PRACTICE: Make a listing (or drawing) of some of the many ways God has been with you throughout your life, especially in the times of fear, burden, and challenges.

ADVENT PRAYER: *You might want to use the Jewish Dayenu prayer. After each happening in your list of God's presence, pray, "If you only did this for me, it would have been enough."*

Song of Songs 2:8–14 or Zephaniah 3:14–18a; Luke 1:39–45

Presen(ts)ce

Mary traveled to the hill country in haste to a town of Judah.

LUKE 1:39

I arrived at my niece's at 7:15 AM. Surprised to see my great-nephew already up, I asked him why he was awake so early. Tyler answered, "I was waiting for you." Often our presence is a gift we give each other.

Today's gospel relates the tender story of another arrival at a relative's home: Mary's trip to be with her cousin Elizabeth. Our physical presence is the best gift we give one another.

Theologian Parker Palmer tells that, during his depression, his friend came every day and massaged his feet. Parker credits Bill with helping to save his life: "He rarely said a word. Unafraid to accompany me in my suffering, he made me less afraid of myself. He was present—simply and fully present."

Our opportunities for presence might not be as dramatic as Mary and Elizabeth's or as extravagant as Parker Palmer's friend. It might be as simple as my time with Tyler. Yet, we never know how our attentive presence might affect a person's life.

DAILY PRACTICE: During this season of presents, how might you focus on presence—the gift of time rather than the gift of things? Make extraordinary memories from ordinary moments. Enjoy the presence of one another more than the presents under the tree.

ADVENT PRAYER: *God of Never-ending Presence, nudge me to attentive presence with everyone I meet today.*

Micah 5:1–4a; Hebrews 10:5–10; Luke 1:39–45

You First

Mary...entered the house of Zechariah and greeted Elizabeth.

LUKE 1:39–40

On Christmas day several years ago, as I was arriving at my brother's home, my niece's family drove up at the same time. As we got out of our cars, five-year-old Tyler ran over to me. I expected him to say, "Guess what Santa brought me!" or "Wait till you hear all the things I got!" Instead, he excitedly said, "Hi, Aunt Janet! Have you been having a good Christmas?"

This simple encounter doesn't compare to the visit of Mary to Elizabeth; yet, perhaps there is one similarity: putting others first.

Amid today's busyness and many responsibilities, it's often normal to find ourselves thinking first about our needs. Do the gospels call us to a different priority? What model does Mary give us—as she traveled during her pregnancy—to respond to her cousin, seeing Elizabeth's needs before her own?

DAILY PRACTICE: As you meet each person today, interestedly ask, "Have you been having a good day?" You might also consider calling, emailing, or texting some family members or friends to ask how they are.

ADVENT PRAYER: *Caring and Interested God, help me to be like you. Don't let me get so caught up in all my concerns (even though they are important to you) that I neglect those around me. Help me see and respond to others' joys, hopes, disappointments, and needs first.*

Malachi 3:1–4, 23–24; Luke 1:57–66

Treasury of Blessings

All who heard these things took them to heart.

LUKE 1:66

In *A Christmas Carol*, Dickens wrote: "Reflect upon your present blessings—of which every [person] has many." The author Margaret Wheatley said: "Without reflection, we go blindly on our way, creating more unintended consequences, and failing to achieve anything useful."

The relatives and neighbors who gathered to celebrate the birth of John were filled with questions about the naming of the infant; they rejoiced when Zechariah's speech was returned to him. The gospel tells us that they shared these astonishing events with others, reflecting on them and treasuring them in their hearts.

The power of memory, of treasuring events and people in our hearts! In these ending Advent days and the celebration of Christmas, let's treasure what matters most. Let's not sweat the small stuff but appreciate the blessings that surround us. Let's not miss the moments of grace in the many ways God is with us. Let's not lose the opportunity to lock away treasures in our hearts from our moments with friends, family, and those to whom we've reached out during this season.

DAILY PRACTICE: At the end of each day, pause and reflect: What did I experience today that I want to treasure in my heart? Because of that memory, how will I live tomorrow?

ADVENT PRAYER: *God our Greatest Treasure, help me to treasure in my heart your constant, incredible blessings.*

2 Samuel 7:1–5, 8b–12, 14a, 16; Luke 1:67–79

Weaving Trusting Hope

*"...because of the tender mercy of our God
by which the daybreak from on high will visit us."*

LUKE 1:78

Hiding in a cave, a soldier prayed that he would be saved. He noticed a spider weaving a web over the opening of the cave. As the enemy approached, searching the caves, they skipped his cave, thinking that no one had entered in quite a while—because of the web.

Given today's challenges—illness, selfishness, mistrust, contempt, violence—we might think it is unrealistic to pray a prayer as trusting as the soldier's, a prayer as hopeful as Zechariah's, in today's gospel.

Yet, who are we? What are we hoping for, longing for? Zechariah's prayer is a summary of our desires, the Christmas Good News: God comes in compassion. "You are not alone. I am Emmanuel: God-with-you. Nothing is impossible with me."

Do we, then, do our part? Do we look for hopeful signs in the world? Rather than perpetuating negativity, do we recognize the good? How are we weaving peace and goodness throughout our part of the world? What are we doing to bring kindness and compassion wherever we are?

DAILY PRACTICE: During this coming week, weave one act of goodness and peace in your world (in addition to the giving of material gifts).

ADVENT PRAYER: *Blessed be the Lord, the God of Israel, for he has visited and brought redemption to his people.*

VIGIL: *Isaiah 62:1–5; Acts 13:16–17, 22–25; Matthew 1:1–25*

Christmas throughout the Year

"They shall name him Emmanuel, which means 'God is with us.'"

MATTHEW 1:23

"Martin the Cobbler" is Leo Tolstoy's story about a lonely shoemaker who is promised, in a dream, that Christ will come to visit. The next day, Martin rises early, gets his shop ready, and waits. The only one who shows up in the morning is an old beggar asking for rest. Martin gives him a room he had prepared for Jesus. The only one to appear in the afternoon is an older woman asking for food. He gives her the food he had prepared for Jesus. As evening comes, a lost boy wanders by. Martin takes him home, afraid all the while that he will miss the Christ. That night he asks the Lord, "Where were you? I waited all day for you."

The Lord replies: "Three times I came to your friendly door. I was the beggar with bruised feet. I was the woman to whom you gave food. I was the child on the street."

Christ is always closer than we imagine. The reality of Christmas—God with us—is happening every day if we pay attention.

DAILY PRACTICE: Begin a journal for 2025, each day completing this sentence: *Today I saw/encountered Jesus when...*

CHRISTMAS DAY PRAYER: *Emmanuel, God-with-Us, your very name reminds me of your comfort and your challenge. As I live the Holy Year of Hope, help me see you everywhere.*